How Things Grow

From Caterpillar

to Butterfly

Sally Morgan

Chrysalis Children's Books

First published in the UK in 2002 by

Chrysalis Children's Books
    An imprint of Chrysalis Books Group Plc
The Chrysalis Building, Bramley Rd, London W10 6SP

Copyright © Chrysalis Books Group Plc 2002
Text by Sally Morgan

ISBN 1 84138 370 8

British Library Cataloguing in Publication Data for this book is available from the British Library.

Series editor: Jean Coppendale
Designer: Angie Allison
Picture researcher: Sally Morgan and Terry Forshaw
Consultants: Bethan Currenti

Printed in Hong Kong

10 9 8 7 6 5 4 3 2 1

Picture acknowlwdgements:
All Photography Chrysalis Images/Robert Pickett with the exception of:
Front cover (main), 21 & 31 NHPA/Stephen Dalton; Title Page, front cover (inset) & 26 Papilio/Robert Pickett; 5 Premaphotos Wildlife/Ken Preston-Mafham; 8 & 28 (TR) OSF/J.A.L. Cooke; 13 Papilio/Robert Pickett; 20 NHPA/Dr. Eckart Pott; 22 & 28 (BL) Ecoscene/Kjell Sandved; 23 (T) Ecoscene, (B) Premaphotos Wildlife/Ken Preston-Mafham; 24 Papilio/Dennis Johnson; 25 Ecoscene/Wayne Lawler; 27 Papilio/Laura Sivell.

Contents

What is a butterfly?

A butterfly is an **insect**. Its body is made up of three parts – a head, **thorax** and **abdomen**. It has six legs and two pairs of brightly coloured wings. The life cycle of the butterfly is made up of four parts – egg, **caterpillar** or larva, **pupa** and adult.

The monarch butterfly has orange and black wings with white spots.

A caterpillar looks very different from an adult butterfly. This is the caterpillar of the red dagger wing butterfly.

The caterpillar does not look anything like an adult butterfly. The change from a caterpillar to an adult is called **metamorphosis** (meta-more-fo-sis). This word means 'change in body shape'.

Laying eggs

The egg is only a few millimetres long. It has a tough shell with ridges.

The female monarch butterfly lays her eggs in late spring and early summer. The eggs are laid on leaves that the caterpillars like to eat. This is their foodplant.

The monarch butterfly lays her eggs on the milkweed plant. Only a few of the eggs will **hatch**. Many of the eggs will be eaten by birds and insects. Others are killed by disease.

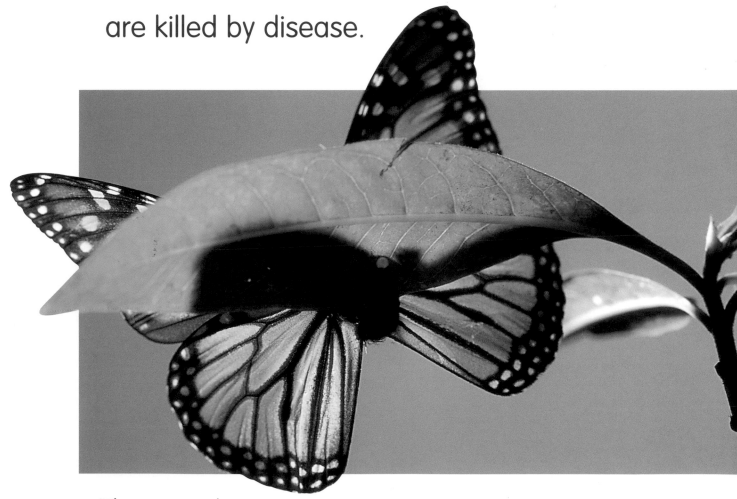

The monarch butterfly attaches her egg to the leaf with a quick-drying glue, which she makes inside her body.

From egg to caterpillar

The eggs hatch after about one week. A caterpillar hatches by pushing its head out through the shell. Then the rest of the body follows.

The caterpillar pushes its way out of the egg.

The caterpillar eats the old shell of the egg.

The newly hatched caterpillar is just a few millimetres long, but it grows quickly. The old shell does not go to waste. It is the first thing the caterpillar eats. Then the caterpillar starts to eat leaves.

The caterpillar of the monarch butterfly has a colourful body of black, white and yellow stripes.

The caterpillar

By the time the caterpillar is fully grown it will be about 7 cm long.

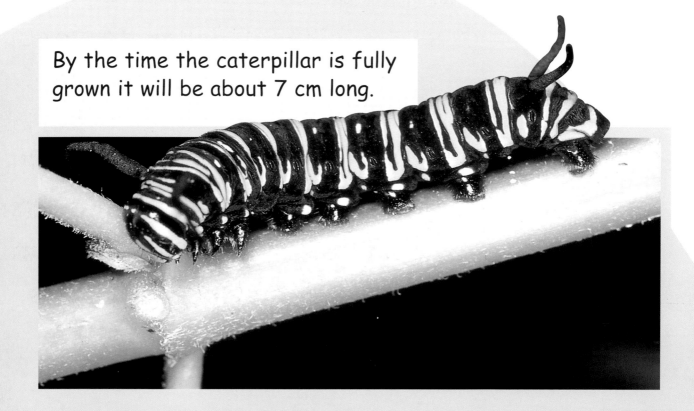

The caterpillar's body is made up of many parts called **segments**. It has a head, a thorax and an abdomen. Caterpillars eat all day and grow very quickly. They have six small eyes on their head and a pair of jaws.

A caterpillar has six pointed legs which are joined to the thorax. It also has four pairs of **prolegs** attached to the abdomen. These are not proper legs. Each proleg ends in a **sucker**. There is a pair of suckers at the end of its body. The suckers help the caterpillar to grip stems and leaves.

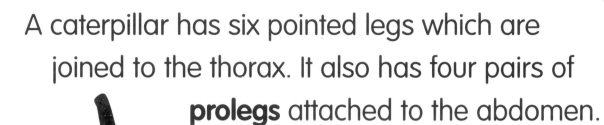

The jaws of the caterpillar are strong and sharp to rip through leaves.

Self-defence

Many animals like to eat caterpillars.
So caterpillars have to find ways to
avoid being eaten. Some caterpillars
are green and brown so that you cannot
see them against leaves and twigs.

The yellow and black stripes along the
body of the monarch butterfly caterpillar
are a warning to other animals to stay
away. If this does not work, it waves
the long black stalks behind its head.

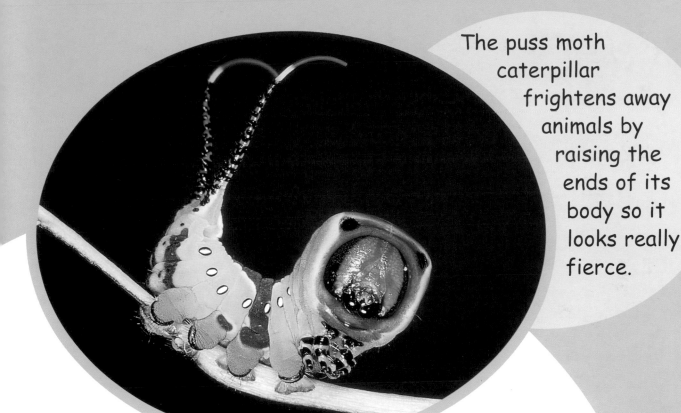

The puss moth caterpillar frightens away animals by raising the ends of its body so it looks really fierce.

Some caterpillars try to scare away animals by making themselves look larger or by waving parts of their body at the approaching animal. Others have **poisons** in their body which make other animals ill. The caterpillar of the monarch butterfly is poisonous. Their brightly coloured bodies are a warning to animals that they taste nasty and should not be eaten.

Time for change

The caterpillar has attached itself to the underside of a leaf using silk threads.

After about three weeks the caterpillar reaches full size and stops feeding. It is ready to become a pupa.

The caterpillar attaches itself to the lower side of a leaf or stem.

The skin of the caterpillar turns into a pupal case.

During the pupal stage, the colour of the pupal case turns from bright green to blue.

Its skin hardens and becomes a pupal case. It stays like that for several weeks. Inside the case major changes are under way. The body of the caterpillar is broken down and changed into the shape of a butterfly. This change is called metamorphosis.

It is just possible to see the body and wings of the new butterfly inside.

A new butterfly

The butterfly emerges from the pupal case.

Now the butterfly is ready to come out from its case. Movements can be seen inside the pupal case. Suddenly the case splits open and the butterfly appears.

The butterfly hangs by its legs from the twig. Its wings are still crumpled.

Slowly the wings open out.

Its wings are **crumpled** and its body is damp. It has to stretch out its wings so that they can harden and dry. It may be two hours before the butterfly is ready to fly away.

The wings are fully open and dry. This butterfly is ready to fly away.

Feeding

A butterfly lands on a flower to feed on nectar.

Butterflies feed on liquid food. One of their favourite foods is **nectar**. This is the sugary liquid made by plants. Butterflies also feed on the sugary juices of fallen fruits such as apples.

When a butterfly is not feeding, its feeding tube is coiled up under its head.

A butterfly sucks up the liquid nectar using a long feeding tube. The tube is very long and it can reach deep into a flower to find the nectar.

When it wants to feed, it extends its feeding tube into the flower.

Surviving winter

The butterflies gather together in large numbers on special trees where they spend the winter.

Butterflies need warm weather. If the weather is too cold, they cannot fly. Many butterflies spend the winter in hiding places where they stay safe and warm. The monarch butterfly spends the summer in central and northern parts of the United States and Canada.

In autumn, the butterflies fly south to California and Mexico where it is warmer. The butterflies come together and rest on special trees called **roosts**. They spend the winter in these trees. In spring, when it gets warmer the butterflies fly north again.

The monarch butterfly is a strong flier and can travel as far as 130 kilometres in just one day.

Finding a mate

Most butterflies live on their own. But they have to find a **mate** in order to **breed**. Female butterflies release a smelly substance into the air as they fly around. Male butterflies have a good sense of smell. They can detect the smell of the female in the air.

A male and female monarch butterfly hang from a flower as they mate.

Moths have large, feathery **antennae**. They also have an excellent sense of smell.

The male follows this smell to the female. Sometimes, when a male and female butterfly meet, they do a dance. They may fly round and round in a spiral, or flash their wings at each other.

This male heliconid butterfly hovers above a female butterfly. He is trying to attract her.

Who eats butterflies?

The black redstart has to catch many caterpillars each day to feed its hungry chicks.

Many different types of animal eat butterflies and caterpillars, including birds, spiders and reptiles. Many garden birds catch caterpillars, which they take back to their nests to feed their young.

Spiders often trap butterflies in their webs. The butterfly flies into the web and become tangled in the sticky threads. Lizards may also catch butterflies as they rest on the ground.

This yellow crab or flower spider has caught a caper white butterfly.

The butterfly family

Bird wing butterflies are among the largest and most colourful of butterflies.

Butterflies are found all over the world – almost anywhere where plants grow. There are more than 20,000 different types of butterfly. Some have wings that are a dull brown colour, but others have brilliant yellow or orange coloured wings or dazzling blues and greens.

In fact, all the colours of the rainbow can be seen on butterfly wings. The largest and most colourful butterflies are found in the tropical parts of the world, especially in **tropical rainforests**.

Many of the butterflies that are found in woodlands have drab brown wings that blend in with dead leaves and twigs on the ground.

The life cycle

1 The eggs of the monarch butterfly are laid on a leaf.

2 About one week later, the eggs hatch into a caterpillar.

8 In spring and early summer the monarch butterflies mate and the female lays her eggs.

7 The adult butterfly feeds on nectar.

3 The caterpillar feeds on leaves and grows quickly.

4 After a few weeks, the caterpillar is fully grown and it changes into a pupa.

6 The pupa splits and an adult butterfly comes out.

5 Inside the pupa, the body of the caterpillar is changed into an adult butterfly.

Glossary

abdomen The third part of an insect's body, behind the head and thorax.

antenna (plural antennae) The feelers of an insect. These help the insect find its way around.

breed To produce offspring.

caterpillar An early stage in the life of a butterfly, a caterpillar looks very different from an adult butterfly. It spends its time feeding and growing.

crumpled Creased or crushed.

hatch To come out of an egg.

insect An animal with six legs and a body made up of a head, thorax and abdomen.

mate One of a pair of animals that come together to breed.

metamorphosis A change in body shape or appearance – for example, when a caterpillar turns into an adult butterfly.

nectar The sugary liquid produced by flowers. Many insects feed on nectar.

poisons Harmful substances.

prolegs Fleshy parts attached to a caterpillar's abdomen that help it to hold on to plants.

pupa A stage in the life cycle of a butterfly during which it changes from a caterpillar into an adult.

roosts Places such as trees, where animals gather and spend the night or winter.

segments The name given to the different sections of the body of an animal such as a worm or insect.

sucker A pad which sticks firmly to the surface of something.

thorax The part of an insect's body, to which the legs and wings are attached.

tropical rainforests Thick forests that grow in areas on either side of the Equator, where it is warm and wet for all or most of the year.

index